It's Salad Time! Chef 7 Star

Equipment you will need for this book

*Cheese cutter, which I will refer to as a vegetable peeler.

*Blender, any regular sized model will work.

*Large bowl and small bowl

*Large Sharpe knife and spoon

*Cutting board

Shopping list/ groceries to have on hand:

Purple onions

Fresh garlic cloves

Large tomatoes with green stem still on

Firm Zucchini

Brown small mushrooms

Fresh Spinach

Red and Yellow bell peppers

Romaine lettuce or an Red leaf lettuce

Purple cabbage

White cabbage

Avocados

Carrots (medium sized to large)

Flax seeds fresh no roasted

Almond slices non roasted

Raw cashews

Dried basil

Italian herb blend

Sea salt

Black pepper

Crushed red peppers

Cayenne pepper

Honey

Lemons

Filtered/ spring water

Olive oil

- Pay attention when handling sharp knifes in the kitchen!

- Make these recipes uniquely yours once you learn to create them from instruction in this book.

I created this book to provide simple instruction for the creation of salads. I love instructing classes and Introducing the deliciousness of salads to humanity. My love for salads was introduced by my husband Artis Hinson. I changed my habits from eating only processed foods to incorporating more salads each day! Changing my lifestyle habits was not easy and now I strive to help others transition into more salads.

All recipes in this book are diary free, gluten free, soy free and even "pasta/noodle" free. Some recipes may refer to "noodles or pasta", yet it is just to describe the similar appearance of the fruit and/or vegetable.

I hope you enjoy this book and discover the wonderful world of fresh salads and experience the magic of how delicious salads can be.

It is my mission to inspire a beautiful relationship between salads and humanity.

If you seek more comforting salad options, including nuts and seeds please check out my 1st recipe book, "Wow! That's RAW!" available on my website and on Amazon.

http://7starlightfoods.webs.com/

Thank you for your support!

Italian Flax

It's Salad Time recipe book, by Chef 7 Star

prep time
10 minutes

serves
2 to 3

things you need

Dressing

1/2 cup
Olive oil

1 tbsp
honey

1 teaspoon
Sea salt

1/2 squeezed
Lemon

1 TBSP

Italian herb blend

3 cloves
garlic

1 teaspoon

Crushed red peppers

Salad

2 bunches

Cleaned red leaf lettuce

1 shaved

Carrot

1/4 Of small

Chopped purple onion

1sheet of
Torn nori sea weed sheet

1 TBSP

Flax seeds/ to be sprinkled

over top

Blend dressing ingredients together in the blender for about 3 minutes..

If you feel more or less of any ingredient should be used , repeat and perfect this recipe for you.

You will not use the entire herb oil dressing on the salad. Once you blend your salad in a bowl, apply 1 small spoon of this dressing at a time and continue to add to your liking and save the remaining dressing in a pint jar or other air tight container. This dressing does not need to be refrigerated.

Once you have added the amount of dressing your desire, sprinkle the salad with flax seeds

here's how to switch it up!

Italian Salad Rolls

What you will need

Nori sheets

Salad from the previous page with choice amount of dressing

Next:

Roll salad into the sea weed and seal with water. (keep a small cup of water to the side to help seal ends)

Smear a bit of water on the outside of the nori and sprinkle flax seeds on the rolls for added crunch.

Carefully using a sharp knife slice the rolled salad into pieces.

Switch it up again!

Herbed Spinach and Tomato salad

What you will need

2 bunches of Spinach

2 medium sized slicing tomatoes

Next:

Add to a large bowl 2 bunches of cleaned spinach and 2 chopped tomatoes

Use the Italian dressing from page 4 and add as much or little as you like

Blend salad together with a large stirring spoon and allow to marinate for about 1 hour before eating and enjoy!

...and again! Great for parties!

Cucumber and cherry tomato pickers

What you will need

1 large cucumber sliced and peeled

1 container of organic cherry tomatoes

Tooth picks

Next:

Slice peeled cucumber into equal sized 1 inch thick pieces

Slice cherry tomatoes into 3 pieces

Use the Italian dressing from page 4 and add about 3 large spoons of herb dressing (be sure to shake dressing to allow dispersion of herbs in the oil).

Marinate the cucumbers and tomatoes in a bowl for about 3 hours

Then start to put each tomato and cucumber on the tooth pick (refer to photo)

Serve and enjoy!

Avocado and Tomtoms

Avocado and Tomato Stackers

<u>What you will need</u>

1 large tasty tomato sliced

1 avocado peeled and without seed

10 black pitted olives chopped

Italian dressing from page 4 in this book.

<u>Next:</u>

Layer tomato and avocado (like photo above)

Top layers with chopped olives then drizzle Italian dressing over top

Quick, simple and super delicious!

Italian Dressing ...one more time!

Olive for salad

<u>What you will need</u>

10 sliced green olives without seeds

1 large slicing tomato (I prefer those bought still with the stem intact) chopped into 1 inch pieces

1 large cucumber sliced into 1 inch pieces, cut into halves

Italian dressing from page 3 ... add as much as you desire be sure not to make the salad too oily

<u>Next:</u>

Blend all chopped ingredients and add dressing: viola, a super flavorful salad. Enjoy

View photo on the left.

To create even more with this salad, place salad on top of a cabbage leaf

Serve and enjoy!

It's Salad Time, Chef 7 Star

Oriental Salad

Oriental Salad

It's Salad Time recipe book, by Chef 7 Star

prep time
10 minutes

serves
2 to 3

things you need

Dressing

1/2 cup
Wheat free Tamari

1 1/2 tbsp
Honey

1/2 teaspoon
Sea salt

1/2 squeezed
Lemon

1 TBSP

Water (filtered)

1 clove
Garlic minced

1 teaspoon

Crushed red peppers

Salad

2 Bunches

Cleaned spinach

1 shaved

Carrot

1/4 Chopped

Purple onion

1/2 chopped
Red pepper diced

1/4 cup
Purple cabbage
chopped

1 TBSP

Almonds

over top

Blend dressing ingredients together in a bowl with a fork or whisk, for about 1 minute. Taste always!

If you feel more or less that any ingredient should be used , repeat and perfect this recipe for yourself.

You may not need to use the entire oriental dressing on this salad. But you can save it for other recipes.

In a bowl blend all salad ingredients together.

Next add dressing over the salad. Start by adding a spoon at a time and mix until you get the consistency of your choice..

Once you have added the amount of dressing desired, sprinkle the salad with almonds as the finishing touch and enjoy! (photo next page)

What else to do with left over oriental dressing?

My favorite oriental dressed kale with almond salad

Now you see how awesome the spiralizer is, as we are going to use it again for this recipe.

What you will need

1 large bunch of cleaned kale removed from stem

1/2 red pepper sliced

Add thin slices of purple onion 1/4 of small onion

1 whole carrot, cleaned and peeled

Oriental dressing from page 9

1 tablespoon of sliced almonds

1. Add cleaned kale to a bowl and combine sliced onion, and red bell pepper

2. Next add oriental dressing 1 spoon at a time to your liking and stir with large spoon. Allow salad to sit for about 30 minutes to soak up all the flavor.

3. Add to plates and enjoy!

Feeds about 2-3 large portions

Mushroom and spinach marinated salad

It's Salad Time, Chef 7 Star

What to do with left over oriental dressing?

Mushrooms please

What you will need

2 large sliced brown mushrooms (clean well and slice into 1 inch pieces)

2 bunches of cleaned spinach (I like to clean and rinse with warm water squeezing the spinach to soften)

2 tablespoons of minced purple or white onion

1 minced clove of garlic

1/2 sliced red pepper

1/2 sliced yellow bell pepper

1/2 sliced green bell pepper

1 hand full of chopped almonds (also soak in the oriental dressing)

Oriental dressing from page 12, add the amount of your desire to coat (marinate) all ingredients

Allow mushrooms and peppers to marinate for about 4 hours, in a warm space near a window, dehydrator or over night (if over night the space does not need to be warm)

Mushrooms will shrink when they have absorbed marinade/dressing

Marinate spinach until leaves wither

Next:

Add mushroom pepper mixture atop the spinach, then add soaked almonds and enjoy!

It's Salad Time, Chef 7 Star

What else to do with left over oriental dressing?

food photos

Oriental noodle salad

Yes, this book is all about salads however , you can use vegetables in awesome ways with the use of a vegetable spiralizer. This trusty device which will encourage more creativity with your salads, can be purchased online at amazon.com

What you will need

2 large zucchini (skin peeled off)

1 crown of cleaned broccoli pieces

2 tablespoons of minced purple or white onion

1 minced clove of garlic

1 peeled carrot

1. spiralize the zucchini noodles

2. Allow broccoli, carrots, onions, and minced garlic to marinate in Oriental dressing for about 4 hours

3. Add noodles (don't stir noodles too much or they will

turn into water) to the marinated veggies

Serve and enjoy .

Feeds about 2-3 large portions

It's Salad Time, Chef 7 Star

What else to do with left over oriental dressing?

Oriental noodle salad with spinach and mushrooms

So for a more satisfying twist on the oriental salad, we are gong to add spinach and mushrooms!

What you will need

10 pieces of brown mushrooms cleaned and sliced

1 bunch of spinach cleaned and squeezed

1 tablespoon of minced purple onion

1 teaspoon of minced garlic (about 1 clove)

2 medium sized zucchini peeled

1. spiralize the zucchini noodles in separate bowl

2. Allow mushrooms, spinach, onions, and garlic to marinate in oriental dressing for about 3-4 hours, in a separate bowl from noodles

3. Add noodles (don't stir noodles too much or they will turn into water) to the 4 hour marinated veggies .

Serve and enjoy .

Feeds about 2-3 large portions

It's Salad Time, Chef 7 Star

We're on a roll! When in need of change, roll it!

It's Salad Time, Chef 7 Star

What else to do with left over oriental dressing?

food photos

7 Star food photos

Oriental noodle salad rolls

Use the already prepared recipe from the previous page to create these super easy delicious bites of love!

1. Place oriental noodle salad inside of nori (as pictured on the left)

Be sure to not gather too much sauce as you place veggies into the nori for rolling.

You also have the option to roll salad without dressing and use dressing as a dipping sauce on the side.

Have a small cup of water on the side to use for sealing ends of the nori, once the salad is placed inside.

2. Allow 1-2 minutes for roll ends to seal after applying water for sealing. To seal nori once salad is placed inside, moisten entire free end of nori with water and roll salad in nori toward free end. Gently press and lay on sealed end until secure.

3. Next be careful and use a cutting board and sharp knife to slice nori into even pieces. Pieces should not be too large but to your liking.

4. place rolls on plate and enjoy,

It's Salad Time, Chef 7 Star

What else to do with left over oriental dressing?

Oriental carrot noodle salad

Now you see how awesome the spiralizer is, we are going to use it again in this recipe.

What you will need

2 large carrots

2 teaspoons of dried sea weed (wakame)

Oriental dressing from page 12

1 large crown of cleaned, separated broccoli

1. spiralize the carrots into noodles and add them to a large bowl

2. Next toss in the clean, separated broccoli and wakami pieces

3. Add oriental dressing by the spoon full as desired

4. You can stir carrot noodles more than zucchini noodles because they are more durable.

Add to plates and enjoy!

Feeds about 2-3 large portions

It's Salad Time, Chef 7 Star

Collard Green Salad

Collard Salad

It's Salad Time recipe book, by Chef 7 Star

prep time
10 minutes

serves
2 to 3

things you need

Dressing

1 teaspoon
Honey

1/2 teaspoon
Sea salt

1/2 squeezed
Lemon

1 TBSP

Olive oil

1 teaspoon

Crushed red pepper flakes

1 clove
Garlic minced

1 TBSP

Filtered water

Salad

6 leaves

Cleaned collard greens

removed from the stem .

and shopped into small thin pieces.

2 Tablespoons

Chopped purple onion

To create this super simple recipe

1.blend all Ingredients of the salad and dressing into the same bowl and stir.

2.Cover and allow mixture to marinate; best over night for super soft collards.

*For extra tang add about 4 chopped sundried tomatoes to your salad before serving.

Spiced Simplicity

Spiced Salad

It's Salad Time recipe book, by Chef 7 Star

prep time
10 minutes

serves
2 to 3

things you need

Dry Spice Blend

1 teaspoon
Sea salt

1/2 teaspoon
Black pepper

1 Lemon
Fresh Squeezed without seeds

1/4 Teaspoon

Cayenne pepper

You will not use the entire mixture on this salad you will sprinkle this on top of your finished salad.

Salad

12 whole

Green olives

1 large

Chopped tomato

1 large

Cleaned and sliced

Cucumber

1 small

Radish sliced thin

2 bunches

Romaine lettuce chopped

2 cloves

Minced garlic

1.Add all salad ingredients to the same bowl

2. Squeeze lemon juice over salad.

3.Next just sprinkle the dry spice blend over salad

(be care not to use too much because cayenne is spicy)

You can also use your favorite natural dry spice seasoning over your salad, if your are in a hurry.

Super Simple

Super Simple

It's Salad Time recipe book, by Chef 7 Star

prep time
10 minutes

serves
2 to 3

things you need

Dressing

2
Lemon's juiced without seeds

2
Pinches of seas salt

2
Pinches of black pepper

Salad

2 Bunches

Cleaned romaine

chopped into pieces

1/4 Chopped

Purple onion

1 clove
Garlic minced

2 tomato
2 chopped tomatoes

1 whole
Avocados with seed removed Chopped into chunks

1. Combine the salad ingredients into a bowl
2. Next pour the lemon juice over top of the salad
3. Follow up by sprinkling the salt and pepper over top
4. Now this super simple delicious salad is ready to serve!

Enjoy!

Non-dairy Cheese Recipe

This "cheese" is great for sandwiches, dipping, pizza and even more!

1 cup soaked cashews (soak cashews for about 6 hours)

½ cup water (Generally 1 cup nuts/seeds to ½ cup water)

1 teaspoon salt

½ teaspoon garlic

½ teaspoon onion powder

1 tablespoon honey

1 lemon squeezed without seeds (use liquid only)

Blend ingredients until smooth (about 3-4 mins)

This will make 1 cup of "cheese". This "cheese" will last about 1 week.

Tomato dressing recipe

1 cup sundried tomato

2 cups of water

1 tablespoon of olive oil

2 cloves of minced garlic

1 tablespoon of chopped onion

1 tablespoon of honey

½ teaspoon of salt (add more or less)

Juice of 1 lemon

Blend until smooth (about 3-4 minutes)

Makes about 2 cups marinara. This will last for about 1 week

Salad lasagna?

Salad Lasagna

It's Salad Time recipe book, by Chef 7 Star

prep time
10 minutes

serves
2 to 3

things you need

Dressing

2/3 cup
Tomato dressing recipe
from PAGE 27

2/3 cup
Cashew cheese from
recipe on page 26

Salad

2 Bunches

Cleaned romaine

chopped into pieces

1/4 Chopped

purple onion

1 clove
garlic minced

1 tomato
Sliced and diced into
1inch pieces

1 tomato
Sliced into half moons
about 1/2 inch to 1 inch
Thick (these will go on top)

1. Take chopped, cleaned romaine and spread it into a bowl.

2. Next add the chopped onion and minced garlic

3. Then add chopped tomato diced into pieces

4. Next spread the cashew cheese over the top evenly

5. Top the cashew cheese with tomato dressing spreaded evenly

6. Lastly add the sliced half moon tomato's to the last visual layer of this salad lasagna. If you have any minced garlic left, then sprinkle some to compete this dish. I even sprinkle a little black pepper over this dish for added spice. You may add chunks of avocado too. (photo below)

Salad Lasagna with avocado

Recipe previous page add avocado chunks and black pepper.

Wow! That's Salad Lasagna

WoW! That's Salad Lasagna

It's Salad Time recipe book, by Chef 7 Star

prep time
10 minutes

serves
2 to 3

things you need

Dressing

1 1/2 cup
Tomato dressing recipe from page 27

1 1/2 cup
Cashew cheese from recipe on page 26

Salad

2 Zucchini

Cleaned and sliced with

a vegetable peeler

1 bunch

Cleaned spinach

1 large
Sliced tomato sliced into 1 inch circles

1 whole
Avocado sliced into thin pieces

1. Use a pan, something used for lasagana and line it with some of the marinara. Then add a row of zucchini "noodles, like you would lasagna noodles in a neat row.

2. In a separate bowl, mix the cleaned spinach with the cashew cheese, saving some of the cheese for the lasagna. I like to mix the 2 ingredients together until the spinach withers down.

3. Next add marinara evenly to the 1st layer of zucchini.

4. Then add the spinach mixture and a bit of cashew cheese.

5. Top that with slices of avocado and tomato, continuing this process until all layers are complete.

6. Once your lasagna is done, you are ready to eat! Enjoy!

Salads for Soup

Nope not chicken noodle soup

What you will need:

1 pack of vegan vegetable bouillon

1 large firm zucchini peeled and spiralized (refer to page 14)

1 medium spiralized carrot (although you won't use all of the carrot)

1 teaspoon dried basil

1. In a small bowl mix the vegan bouillon with water, until it makes a thick paste. Add more water until it be-come a "soup" consistency. Start out with 2 table spoons of water and add 1 tablespoon at a time until you reach 1 cup of broth. If flavor needs more enhancement add 1/2 of another vegan bouillon.

2. Next add zucchini noodles and carrots (try to get the ratio like the photo above) to the broth.

3. Add 1 teaspoon of dried basil and stir gently (zucchini noodles break easily and can turn into water.)

4. Now you are ready to enjoy! Serves about 2

Mushroom collard soup

<u>What you will need: serves about 2</u>

8 small brown mushrooms, cleaned and sliced into equal parts of about 1/2 inch thick.

1 large collard green leaf, cleaned and minced (view photo)

1 table spoon of minced purple onion

1 garlic clove minced

1 cup of filtered water

1 teaspoon of wheat free tamari (this is a gluten free version of "soy" sauce)

1 teaspoon of sea salt

1. tart to create the broth by adding the tamari, water, collard pieces, sea salt, onion and garlic to a bowl.

2. Next add the mushrooms and allow them to marinate in the broth until they have shrunk and soaked up the sauce.

3. Once the magic of marinating has occurred you are ready to enjoy your soup!

Parsley soup/ herb dressing

Take a blender and combine the following ingredients

- 1/2 bunch of parsley cleaned using stems

- About 1/4 bunch of cilantro cleaned using stems

- The juice of 2 lemons without seeds

- 1 diced tomato

- 1 table spoon of dill seeds

- 1 teaspoon of sea salt (add a bit more if you like)

- Pinch of cayenne pepper or red pepper flakes

- 1 tablespoon of honey

- 1/4 cup of raw sunflower seeds

- 2 ozs of filtered water

Blend all ingredients for about 3 minutes, in a blender until smooth. More water may have to be added if your blender slows down. However blend until smooth!

Green Goddess

Green Goddess

It's Salad Time recipe book, by Chef 7 Star

prep time
10 minutes

serves
2 to 3

things you need

Dressing

1/2 cup
Parsley herb soup, this will
be the dressing PAGE 36

Salad

2 bunches

Cleaned and chopped

romaine lettuce or

salad green of your choice

1/4 onion

Chopped into thin pieces

1 whole large
Avocado sliced into chunks

1.In a large bowl add the cleaned and
chopped romaine with onions. We are gong
to add the avocado last after the dressing.

2.Then pour the 1/2 cup of parsley soup over
the salad and viola!

3. Top this salad with avocado chunks and
enjoy!

For an addition mince some sundried tomatoes to this salad.

Pasta Marinara

Pasta Marinara

It's Salad Time recipe book, by Chef 7 Star

prep time
10 minutes

serves
2 to 3

things you need

Dressing

1/2 cup
Tomato dressing from recipe in this book

Salad

1 bunch

Cleaned spinach

2 whole

Firm zucchini peeled with

vegetable peeler into slices after

removing outer green skin

Then once the green skin is removed

Now take out another bowl

And continue using the veggie

Peeler to create "noodles".

Continue to strip whole zucchini's

If you order a veggie slicer,

this will give you more options

when cutting noodles and creating unique shapes.

1. Add to a large bowl the zucchini slices (we will call these noodles)

2. Pour over the tomato dressing(from recipe in this book)

3. Stir ingredients together

4. Add some black olives minus the seeds to this dish or sprinkle with black pepper to complete!

5. Even add some marinated mushrooms or yellow squash slices,

6. Now this dish is complete enjoy!

Simple Spaghetti

It's Salad Time recipe book, by Chef 7 Star

prep time
10 minutes

serves
2 to 3

things you need

Dressing

1/2 tbsp
Dry basil

2 pinches
Sea Salt

Salad

1 Firm

Zucchini peeled and

spirailized

For more info on

spiralizing ref. page 15

1 large

Tomato sliced

(like in photo)

1. Add spiralized zucchini noodles to a large bowl

2. Next add the sliced tomatoes

3. Sprinkle the dried basil and sea salt to the salad and that's it!

Hearty Spaghetti

Hearty Spaghetti

It's Salad Time recipe book, by Chef 7 Star

prep time
10 minutes

serves
2 to 3

things you need

Dressing

1 Cup
Tomato dressing recipe
From page 27
* add to the tomato
dressing 1 tablespoon of
Italian herb blend and stir.

Salad

2 Firm

Zucchini peeled and

spiralized

For more info on

spiralizing ref. page 15

1/2 half

Sliced green bell pepper

1/2 large

Cucumber sliced and

cut into halves

1/4

Sliced purple onion

1. Add spiralized zucchini noodles to a large bowl

2. Next add the sliced peppers, cucumbers and onion to bowl with 1 cup marinara and stir ingredients together.

3. Next create individual servings of zucchini noodles then sauce, and top with organic cherry tomatoes

Red pepper pastless PASTA!

Red pepper pastaless PASTA

It's Salad Time recipe book, by Chef 7 Star

prep time
10 minutes

serves
2 to 3

things you need

Dressing

2 whole
Red peppers
Diced into pieces

2 cloves
Garlic with skin removed

1/4
Purple onion

1 tablespoon
Honey

1 teaspoon
Sea salt

1/2 tbsp.
Olive oil

1 lemon
Squeezed without seeds

Salad

2 Firm

Peeled and sliced into 4ths

Then 1/2 those 4 pieces and

Chop each piece into

1 inch pieces like

the photo above

1/2 half

Sliced red bell pepper

1/2 half

Sliced green bell pepper

1/4

Sliced purple onion

1. Add to a blender all the dressing ingredients as listed and process until smooth and thick. Taste and add more sea salt if you choose.

2. Add to a large bowl the zucchini pieces

3. Stir in the red pepper dressing (these "noodles" are more durable and can be stirred for longer periods of time to develop flavor)

4. Now this salad is done! Enjoy ~

Avocado Lovers!

Avocado lovers!

Avocado lovers!

It's Salad Time recipe book, by Chef 7 Star

prep time
10 minutes

serves
2

Things you need for a basic recipe, once your learn use your creativity!

Dressing

1 half avocado
Make sure avocado is soft but not over ripened . The inside should be green with no blemishes.

1 clove garlic
Mince garlic

1 teaspoon
Sea salt (add more if you would like)

1/2 lemon
Squeezed without seeds

Salad

1/2 Purple Onion

Chopped like previous page photo.

2 Green peppers

Cleaned and chopped

without the core

like in the photo on the previous

page.

1 Red Pepper

Cleaned and chopped

(refer to previous page for visual)

In a large bowl add:

1. chopped peppers and onions
2. Next add the 1/2 avocado without the outer skin to the bowl with the peppers and onions.
3. Next squeeze 1/2 lemon without seeds
4. Add 1 teaspoon of sea salt
5. Add in 1 clove of garlic mined
6. Stir mixture with a spoon until creamy.
7. Taste and add more salt to fit your desire.

Get creative with this dish and add ingredients like dry or fresh basil, curry powder, masala, or chili powder; the possibilities are endless.

Not so Ranch Salad!

Not so RANCH salad

It's Salad Time recipe book, by Chef 7 Star

prep time
10 minutes

serves
2 to 3

things you need

Dressing

1/2 cup
Not really cheese from page 26

Salad

2 Bunches

Cleaned and chopped

Romaine lettuce or

Salad green of choice

1/2 half

Sliced and diced

red bell pepper

1. In a bowl, place cleaned and chopped romaine

2. Next top the salad with the "cheese" which will act as our "ranch". You may not use the whole 1/2 cup, of cheese as recipe indicates. Add as much as you desire.

3. Top salad with diced red peppers and it's ready!

I always add spice to my salads, so sprinkle crushed red peppers on top or spice your desire.

Pasta-less Alfredo

It's Salad Time recipe book, by Chef 7 Star

prep time	serves
10 minutes	2 to 3

things you need

Dressing

1 cup
Not really cheese from page 26

1 tspn
Dry basil

Salad

2 Sliced

Peeled zucchini sliced

With vegetable peeler

6 sliced

Sun dried tomatoes

1 crown

Cleaned and peeled

Broccoli into small pieces

1 Carrot

Peeled carrot with veggie

peeler

1. Prepare the "pasta" by peeling the green layer off the zucchini . Next slice the zucchini with the vegetable peeler,. Then use a knife and slice each piece into 3's. This will create linguini like shaped "pasta".

2. Next toss in the broccoli pieces, peeled carrot slices and sundried tomatoes in a bowl

3. Add the 1 cup of "cheese" on top and sprinkle with dried basil and stir

4. Now this pasta salad is ready for your enjoyment!

Basil Pesto "Pasta"

Basil Pesto Pasta

It's Salad Time recipe book, by Chef 7 Star

prep time
10 minutes

serves
1

things you need

Dressing

1/2 cup
Not really cheese from the earlier part of this book

1Teaspoon
Dry basil

1leaf fresh basil
Clean and chop

*Add all these ingredients to a blender and blend until integration of ingredients has taken place (about 1-2 mins)

Salad

1 large

Zucchini with the skin removed,

and spiralized in to "noodles".

1 large

Fresh tomato sliced into

Chunks

Step 1: After you have made your basil "cheese" for the pesto set it aside. You may have some left over.

Step 2: Pour about 1/4 cup of basil "dressing" over noodles. And stir lightly til each noodle is covered.

Step 3: Add your tomatoes and fresh chopped basil and enjoy!

Cheezy Spinach

Cheezy spinach

It's Salad Time recipe book, by Chef 7 Star

prep time
10 minutes

serves
2 to 3

things you need

Dressing
1/2 cup
Not really cheese from page 26

Salad
4 hands full

Fresh chopped spinach

1. On a cutting board chop your cleaned spinach into many pieces. To do this you may have to gather the spinach and hold it together tight then chop.

2. Once you have your spinach chopped add to a large bowl.

3. Add the "not really cheese" to your spinach and stir with a large spoon. Be sure to place excess spinach stuck to the spoon back into your bowl.

4. You can allow this mixture to sit and marinate, which will soften the spinach or you can stir for about 3-5 minutes non-stop and this will soften the spinach well.

This recipe works great as a dip or to fill breads or wraps.

Okra ummm hmmmm!

My favorite Okra salad!

It's Salad Time recipe book, by Chef 7 Star

prep time
10 minutes

serves
2 to 3

things you need

Dressing

2 Pinches
Sea salt

2 pinches
Black pepper

Salad

2 fresh

Heirloom tomatoes

work best for this salad

10 okra

Take top off and chop

into 1inch pieces

1 tablespoon

Purple onion minced

1 clove

Minced garlic

Optional! 1 inch piece of

Jalapeno minced

1. In a large bowl add sliced tomato (slice tomato into 1 inch thick half moons)

2. In the same bowl add the okra, minced onions, minced garlic.

3. Stir everything together and sprinkle black pepper and sea salt on top This yummy digestive treat is ready to enjoy!

Yes this salad does get slimy, but embrace it!

The slime is good.

Stuffed okra stew tomato

Okra "stew" salad!

It's Salad Time recipe book, by Chef 7 Star

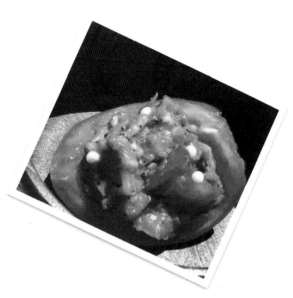

prep time
10 minutes

serves
2 to 3

things you need

Dressing

1 cup
Tomato dressing from Page 27

1 teaspoon
Black pepper

Salad

2 fresh

Heirloom tomatoes

work best for this salad

diced into 1 inch pieces

and another for stuffing

10 okra

Take top off and chop

into 1inch pieces

1 tablespoon

Purple onion minced

1 clove

Minced garlic

Optional! 1 inch piece of

1. In a large bowl add the okra, diced tomatoes, minced onions, minced garlic.

2. Next stir the tomato dressing into the bowl with the veggies . Stir until juices come together to create a "stew" like consistency. A bit of water or orange juice can be used.

3. Next take a large sized tomato cut it in half. Then scoop the inside out(add this inner-core to the stew) .

4. In each half fill it with the stew and enjoy!

This preparation of the okra is less slimy.

Middle Eastern Cauliflower

Middle Eastern Cauliflower

It's Salad Time recipe book, by Chef 7 Star

prep time
10 minutes

serves
2 to 3

things you need

Dressing

1 avocado
Soft and green

1 teaspoon
Choice Masala seasoning

- sea salt to taste, start with 1 teaspoon
- 1/2 lemon squeezed

Salad

1 fresh

Cauliflower

12 Cherry

Tomatoes

8 Olives

Purple onion minced

2 Tablespoons

Minced sweet onion

- 1/2 carrot chopped

1. Take cauliflower and rinse then remove outer leafs.

2. Use a large knife and chop cauliflower into small pieces, which will be easier to dice.

3. Chop cauliflower into small pieces you can also shred with a mandolin, or use a food processor and pulse about 3 times (not too much or cauliflower will be too fine and watery)

4. Once you have your chopped cauliflower add to a large bowl and chop your carrot and white onion according to recipe.

5. Next open your avocado and use only the inside minus the seed and add to cauliflower, next slice cherry tomatoes in 1/2 and add 6 of them to cauliflower and sit them to the side, chop your olives and add them to the cauliflower.

6. Next add 1 teaspoon of your masala spice (which can be found at international markets or Indian food stores) to the cauliflower and veggies in the large bowl, then use a large spoon and mash the avocado into the cauliflower, turning the bowl and stirring until mixed well. Then add 1 teaspoon of sea salt (make sure your masala doesn't have salt already, some come with it.) If that is the case then skip this step. Squeeze 1/2 lemon juice without seeds, stir and enjoy.

Established in 1975
Body Ecology Life Sciences Attunement Center, is dedicated to providing unique personalized service. We ship products for your convenience.

We blend formulas for any condition based on your date of birth from natural herbs. These products include but are not limited to:

- natural Weight off
- herbal detox #1 seller
- pain formula for arthritis
- natural tooth care
- personalized cologne
- books
- colloidal gold and copper
- crystals/stones
- astrological readings
- quality skin care
- herbs and more

Husband wife owners. Mr. and Mrs. Hinson

336 273 7406 www.bodyecol.net

Chef 7 Star brings a comforting new twist on RAW foods!

All gluten free, dairy free recipes; with a little dehydrating to warm things up!

"WoW! That's RAW ?" Will blow your mind with amazing Raw vegan recipes sure to satisfy your every comfort food craving!

http://www.livingsuperfood.com/

Lifeit Cafe
730 South Pleasantburg Drive, Suite L
Greenville, SC 29607
864-402-9231
latrice@lifeitcafe.com
www.lifeitcafe.com